MUGGSY BOGUES

TALL ON TALENT

By Howard Reiser

 Children's Press®
A Division of Grolier Publishing
New York   London   Hong Kong   Sydney
Danbury, Connecticut

Photo Credits

Cover, ©David L. Johnson/Sports Photo Masters, Inc.; 5, ©David L. Johnson/
SportsChrome East/West; 6, 9, 10, ©David L. Johnson/Sports Photo Masters,
Inc.; 11, AP/Wide World; 12, ©David L. Johnson/Sports Photo Masters, Inc.;
15, UPI/Bettmann; 17, ©David L. Johnson/SportsChrome East/West; 18,
AP/Wide World; 21, Focus on Sports; 22, UPI/Bettmann; 25, Courtesy Wake
Forest Sports Information; 26, AP/Wide World; 29, ©Brian Drake/SportsChrome
East/West; 30, AP/Wide World; 31, Focus on Sports; 32, ©David L. Johnson/
Sports Photo Masters, Inc.; 35, AP/Wide World; 36, ©Noren Trotman/Sports
Photo Masters, Inc.; 39, ©David L. Johnson/Sports Photo Masters, Inc.; 40,
AllSport; 43, ©David L. Johnson/SportsChrome East/West; 44 (left), Courtesy
Wake Forest Sports Information; 44 (right), AP/Wide World; 45 (both photos),
46, 47, ©David L. Johnson/Sports Photo Masters, Inc.

Acknowledgments

The author would like to thank librarian Nylah Schneider; NBA coaches Pat
Riley and Mike Dunleavy; former Dunbar High School basketball coach Bob
Wade; Jason Brannon, Assistant Public Relations Director of the Charlotte
Hornets; the Elias Sports Bureau; the Public Relations Department of the
National Basketball Association; former basketball great Walt Frazier; and
sports announcer Marv Albert.

Editorial Staff

Project Editor: Mark Friedman
Design: Herman Adler Design Group
Photo Editor: Jan Izzo

Library of Congress Cataloging-in-Publication Data

Reiser, Howard.
    Muggsy Bogues : tall on talent Time / by Howard Reiser.
      p. cm. – (Sports stars)
    ISBN 0-516-04396-X
      1. Bogues, Tyrone, 1965–   —Juvenile literature. 2. Basketball players—
United States—Biography—Juvenile literature. I. Title. II. Series.
    GV884.B64M84   1996
    796.323'092–dc20   95-33637
    [B]   CIP
                                     AC

MUGGSY BOGUES

TALL ON TALENT

Muggsy Bogues has difficulty looking other basketball players straight in the eye. But this has nothing to do with being shy. It is simply that he is short. He is so short that he does not measure above the waist of most basketball centers. He's so short that many ball boys are taller than he is.

Muggsy Bogues is, indeed, short. He is the shortest man in the history of the National Basketball Association (NBA). At 5' 3", Muggsy competes in a sport dominated by centers who stand over 7 feet tall.

But short stature has not stopped Muggsy. Tyrone Curtis "Muggsy" Bogues is proof that all dreams can be realized and that nothing is impossible.

Muggsy's coach on the Charlotte Hornets, Allan Bristow, says: "People say we are not likely to see another Larry Bird. I say we have a better chance of seeing another [player as good as] Larry Bird than we have of seeing another Muggsy Bogues. What Muggsy has done, nobody has done."

Or listen to Pat Riley, coach of the Miami Heat: "Muggsy Bogues, at 5' 3", is as unique a point guard as was Magic Johnson at 6' 9". Muggsy is a tremendous player. He has defied all odds, has had a fantastic career, and continues to build upon a record of greatness. And he is a wonderful role model for kids."

Muggsy's coach thinks his talent is as unique as that of the great Larry Bird (left).

Muggsy is not as tall as other NBA players, but he is one of the fastest men on any court.

This is what Milwaukee Bucks coach Mike Dunleavy says about Muggsy's abilities on the court: "[He] has so much speed, so much energy. He is excellent at pushing the ball upcourt and at making great passes. He is also so tough on defense, using his speed and energy to disrupt the other team. In addition, Muggsy is a great leader."

Standing with his teammates, it's easy to find Muggsy — he's third from the right.

Muggsy Bogues is proud of his basketball
achievements. But he is not surprised by his
success. He always believed that if he were
given the chance, he would succeed among
the basketball giants. He says, "I always knew
I could play the game of basketball. I always
believed in myself."

Tyrone Bogues was born on January 9, 1965,
to Richard and Elaine Bogues. He was the
youngest of four children. He has two brothers,
Richard and Anthony, and a sister, Sherron.

The Bogueses lived in the Lafayette Court
Housing Project in East Baltimore, Maryland.
It was a rough neighborhood, where violence was
a daily threat. Tyrone, himself, was hit in the
arm and leg by shotgun pellets when he was five
years old. Fortunately, he was not hurt seriously.

Tyrone's love affair with basketball began when he was a young boy. He especially loved to practice dribbling. He enjoyed it so much that he would dribble a basketball with one hand while carrying bags of garbage out of the house with the other. Neighbors looked forward to watching little Muggsy perform this feat.

Tyrone often would accompany his brothers and sister to the playground and the local basketball courts. There, he would ask to be allowed to play with the older boys. They usually answered, "No, Tyrone, you're too small."

Tyrone would get angry, but he tried not to become discouraged. He continued playing basketball as much as he could. He played a lot with his best friend, Reggie Williams. Reggie later became a star basketball player at Georgetown University and in the NBA.

Muggsy's boyhood friend, Reggie Williams, went on to star for Georgetown University.

When he was about nine years old, Tyrone began getting noticed for his excellent basketball skills. It was also about this time that he was given the nickname "Muggsy." The way Tyrone pestered everyone on defense reminded his friend, Dwayne Woods, of a bothersome character in the old *Bowery Boys* movies. Dwayne said, "Tyrone, you're out there mugging everyone!" Since then, Tyrone has been known as "Muggsy."

A year or two later, Muggsy was well known in the Baltimore basketball scene. NBA player David Wingate also grew up in Baltimore. He remembers, "We were about 11 years old when I saw him for the first time before the start of a recreational league game. Muggsy was so little, I wondered, 'Why is he here?'"

Then Wingate saw him play. "Muggsy was so fast, you couldn't find him without a radar."

Muggsy is known for his outstanding play on defense.

Bob Wade was coach of Baltimore's famous Dunbar High School basketball team. He remembers, "Muggsy played with [bigger and older] kids . . . but Muggsy was still the main catalyst on the court. I was very impressed by how he controlled the flow of the game — both offensively and defensively."

Muggsy's athletic skills were not limited to basketball. At the age of 12, he won a citywide Ping-Pong championship and a state junior wrestling championship. In fact, some people felt that Muggsy was too short for basketball and should focus on wrestling. After all, colleges would not offer basketball scholarships to someone who might not grow taller than five feet.

　 ⭐ ⭐ ⭐

Muggsy ignored the doubters and continued
playing basketball. Meanwhile, Dwayne Woods
(who was also short for a basketball player)
became a star player at Dunbar and won a
college basketball scholarship. "Dwayne Woods
inspired me," says Muggsy. "He was my hero."

Dwayne Woods provided Muggsy with a
lot of support during a tough time in his life.
When Muggsy was 12 years old, his father
was sentenced to 20 years in prison on robbery
charges. Fortunately, Muggsy had a wonderful
mother to lean on. He recalls, "She was not only
a mom, but also like a dad. She had faith in me."

After her husband was jailed, Elaine
Bogues studied hard and received her high-
school equivalency diploma. She also worked
as a secretary to keep food on the table and
clothes on her children. Muggsy says that,
thanks to his mother, "We never felt poor.
We never felt deprived."

Reggie Lewis starred with Muggsy on the Dunbar High School basketball team. Lewis (#35) is shown here playing for the Boston Celtics. In 1993, he died suddenly of heart failure.

Muggsy and his friends dreamed of playing
for Dunbar High School. He recalls, "My friends
and I always talked about that while growing
up. We knew that if you had talent and played
at Dunbar, you had a good chance [of] getting
a basketball scholarship."

After his freshman year at Southern High
School, Muggsy was overjoyed when he was
allowed to transfer to Dunbar for the 1981-82
school year. Joining Reggie Williams, David
Wingate, and Reggie Lewis (also a future NBA
star), Dunbar went on to national acclaim. In
Muggsy's two years on the varsity team, Dunbar
won an incredible 59 games without a single loss!
Muggsy was part of two straight city and state
championships. In his senior season, Dunbar
was voted the best high-school basketball team
in the United States.

Says Dunbar Coach Bob Wade: "I feel we were
the best basketball team of all time. And Muggsy
was most responsible for our reaching that level
of greatness. He was my MVP."

$$\bigstar \quad \bigstar \quad \bigstar$$

After graduating from high school, college recruiters pursued Muggsy, even though he was far shorter than most college stars. With Coach Wade's assistance, Muggsy decided to attend Wake Forest University in Winston-Salem, North Carolina. Wade knew that at Wake Forest, Muggsy would get an excellent education, and he would also get a lot of playing time on the basketball team. "Mr. Wade was like a second father to me," says Muggsy.

Muggsy looked forward to his debut season at Wake Forest. He was not at all concerned that he would be the shortest player in the history of the Atlantic Coast Conference.

**Muggsy (#14) in action for the Wake Forest University
Demon Deacons**

As a point guard, Muggsy typically runs the ball downcourt and passes to an open man.

"I had known for a long time I wasn't going to grow taller than the 5-foot range," recalls Muggsy, whose family members are also short. "I didn't spend time thinking about my size."

Muggsy did not start any games in his freshman year. Yet he often made exciting passes and steals as Wake Forest compiled a record of 21-8. They made it to the final eight of the NCAA tournament. And in just one year, Muggsy had become a favorite with the Wake Forest fans.

"When I came off the bench to play, I would receive loud cheers," Muggsy recalls. But the cheers could not erase his disappointment over not having played more often. The next year, however, things were different. Muggsy became the starting point guard. He quickly earned a reputation as a star player.

--- ★ ★ ★ ---

In a nationally televised game on February 2, 1985, Muggsy scored 20 points, with 10 assists and four steals. NBC announcer Al McGuire said, "He's the most impressive player I've seen in forty years of watching basketball."

As Wake Forest finished the regular season with a 15-12 record, Muggsy set school records of 207 assists and 85 steals. The next year, new coach Bob Staak brought a fast-paced style of play to Wake Forest. It was a style perfectly suited to Muggsy's talents. Muggsy continued to excel under Coach Staak, but there was little else to enjoy about the Wake Forest team in Muggsy's final two years in college. While his teammates struggled, Muggsy continued breaking school and conference records. By the end of his college career, Muggsy had set an ACC record with 781 assists. And he led the conference in steals, assists, and minutes played for three consecutive seasons.

NBA Commissioner David Stern congratulates Muggsy on draft day.

None of Muggsy's college thrills could match his glee on June 22, 1987. On that date, the Washington Bullets made him the 12th choice in the first round of the NBA draft. "It was a great, exciting moment," Muggsy recalls. It was made even greater when his high-school teammates, Reggie Williams and Reggie Lewis, also were drafted in the first round. It was the first time three high-school teammates were drafted in the opening round of the NBA draft.

Muggsy soon signed a million-dollar contract to play for the Bullets. One of the first things he did after signing the contract was to buy his mother a new house.

Muggsy in his rookie season with the Washington Bullets

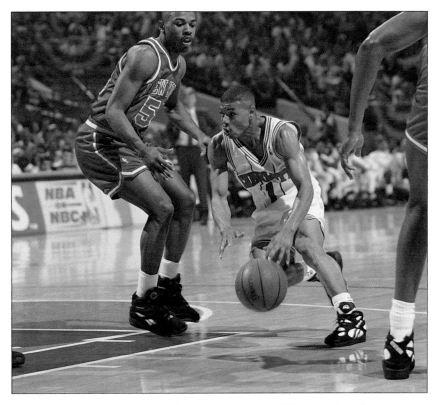

From his first days as a Charlotte Hornet, Muggsy has been a fan favorite.

--- ⋆ ⋆ ⋆ ---

Muggsy's rookie season in the NBA was
difficult. The Bullets were not a very good team.
Team morale was poor. By the end of the season,
Muggsy was playing little, and he admits he lost
confidence in himself.

After the season, the Bullets left Muggsy
unprotected in the expansion draft. The draft
was held so that new, expansion teams could
select players to build their rosters. Muggsy was
selected by the Charlotte Hornets. He thought
this was a wonderful opportunity to re-establish
his reputation as an excellent point guard.

Muggsy soon discovered the drawback of
playing on an expansion team. These teams
are not very good. Charlotte was only 20-62 in
its first year and 19-63 the next year. But the
team was extremely popular in North Carolina,
where basketball had many loyal fans. The
Hornets led the league in attendance their first
year, and Muggsy was one of the home fans'
favorite players.

Still, Muggsy had trouble establishing himself as an everyday starter. He often was the target of unkind words by his own head coach, Dick Harter. Once, when asked about having Muggsy help defend against New York Knicks center Patrick Ewing, Harter responded, "Will a midget really bother Patrick Ewing?"

Harter was replaced in the middle of the 1989-90 season by assistant coach Gene Littles. Muggsy immediately moved into the starting lineup at point guard. He finished the season among the league's leaders in assists and steals. He was voted MVP of the Hornets.

In the NBA, Muggsy found himself up against big challenges.
Here, he attempts to guard the great Michael Jordan.

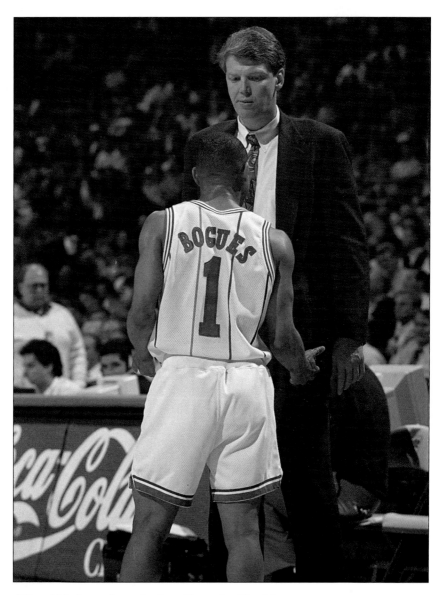

Allan Bristow gives instructions to Muggsy.

$$\star \quad \star \quad \star$$

In the early 1990s, Charlotte began showing improvement. It won 26 games in 1990-91, and then improved to 31-51 in 1991-92 under a new head coach, Allan Bristow. Muggsy played in all 82 games for the first time that year. His 743 assists were fourth-best in the league, and highest in the Eastern Conference. Muggsy had finally established himself as a reliable, everyday point guard in the NBA. He also began to take on the role of team leader. He helped his new rookie teammate, Larry Johnson, ease into the league.

Hornets fans had good reason to celebrate the following season. First, the team added All-American Georgetown center Alonzo Mourning to its roster. Then, it proceeded to post its first winning season ever. The Hornets' 44-38 record in 1992-93 put them in the playoffs for the first time.

In the post-season, Muggsy and his
young teammates shocked everyone when
they defeated the Boston Celtics, three games
to one. Celtics guard Sherman Douglas was
so frustrated by Muggsy's intense defense,
Douglas said, "I wanted to slap him."

The Hornets' post-season success ended
when they lost to the New York Knicks in the
second round. But Charlotte held a parade for
their up-and-coming team. More than 25,000
fans cheered wildly. Nobody signed more
autographs than Muggsy Bogues. "It was
simply great," says Muggsy.

Muggsy threads a pass between Boston Celtics defenders.

Muggsy (5'3") meets Manute Bol (7'7"), who is one of the tallest men in NBA history.

---- ☆ ☆ ☆ ----

Muggsy had been a key player for the Hornets that season. He averaged 10.8 points per game. His 780 assists were fourth-best in the league. And his assists-per-game average was second-best in the NBA — 10.1.

The Charlotte Hornets continue to rise in the standings, and Muggsy Bogues is still their main man on the court. In 1994-95, the team finished only two games out of first place in the Central Division of the Eastern Conference. Muggsy's 11.1 points per game were a career high, and he racked up 675 assists, fifth-best in the league.

Today, Muggsy Bogues has earned the respect of his NBA peers. And fans everywhere love him — especially children. In fact, children often knock on his door, asking whether he can play ball with them. He laughs, "I imagine I am less intimidating [to fans] than a 7-foot player."

★ ★ ★

Although Muggsy often jokes with youngsters, he is always serious when he offers them advice. "I tell them to give themselves a chance. I tell kids that if they study hard, they can make it to college. I tell them that if they are determined, they can make their dreams come true. I am not saying that everyone can make it in the NBA. But I tell them that nothing is impossible, whether it's becoming a basketball player, a fireman, a police officer, or anything else."

Muggsy realizes that many youngsters see him as a hero. "I'm proud to be a role model," he says. "It is an honor to be in the position of helping children — just as I was helped."

The cheers for Tyrone "Muggsy" Bogues will continue for many years to come.

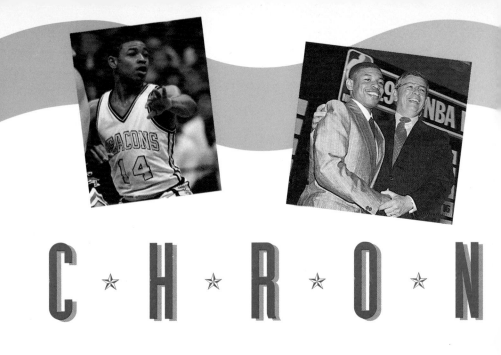

C★H★R★O★N

1965   • January 9: Tyrone Curtis Bogues is born in East Baltimore, Maryland.

1974   • Tyrone is given nickname of "Muggsy."

1977   • Muggsy wins citywide Ping-Pong championship and state junior wrestling championship.

1981-83 • Muggsy attends Dunbar High School and helps its basketball team win two straight city and state championships, as well as achieve a 59-0 record over two seasons.

1983-87 • Muggsy attends Wake Forest University. In his final three seasons, he leads the Atlantic Coast Conference in steals, minutes played, and assists. He graduates from Wake Forest holding seven school basketball records.

O ★ L ★ O ★ G ★ Y

1987 • June 22: Muggsy is drafted by the Washington Bullets in the first round of the NBA college draft.

1988 • June 23: Muggsy is selected by the Charlotte Hornets in the expansion draft.

1991-92 • Muggsy leads the Eastern Conference with 743 assists.

1992-93 • Muggsy averages 10.0 points per game, the first time he is in double figures in scoring average.

1994-95 • Muggsy averages a career high of 11.1 points per game. He becomes the second player in NBA history to achieve more than 600 assists in seven consecutive seasons (the other is all-time assists leader John Stockton).

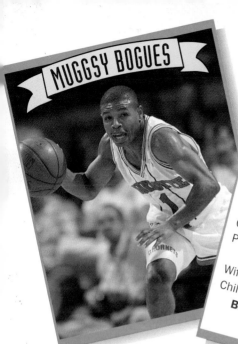

MUGGSY BOGUES

TYRONE CURTIS BOGUES

Nickname **Muggsy**
Place of Birth **East Baltimore, Maryland**
Date of Birth **January 9, 1965**
Height **5' 3"**
Weight **140**
High School **Dunbar (Baltimore)**
College **Wake Forest University**
Pro Teams **Washington Bullets; Charlotte Hornets**
Wife **Kim**
Children **Daughters Tyisha and Brittney; son Ty**

★ NBA STATISTICS ★

Season	Team	Scoring Average	Rebounds	Steals	Assists	Assists Per Game
1987-88	Washington	5.0	136	127	404	5.1
1988-89	Charlotte	5.4	165	111	620	7.8
1989-90	Charlotte	9.4	207	166	867	10.7
1990-91	Charlotte	7.0	216	137	669	8.3
1991-92	Charlotte	8.9	235	170	743	9.1
1992-93	Charlotte	10.0	298	161	711	8.8
1993-94	Charlotte	10.8	313	133	780	10.1
1994-95	Charlotte	11.1	257	103	675	8.7
Total (8 seasons)		**8.43**	**1,827**	**1,108**	**5,469**	**8.57**

About the Author

Howard Reiser has been a well-known New York City newspaper reporter, feature writer, political columnist, and City Hall bureau chief. He has also worked as a labor news writer and editor. Reiser covered the major news stories in New York City for more than 25 years. Today, he is a political speechwriter.

Reiser is the author of ten books for young people. He has written biographies of Nolan Ryan, Scottie Pippen, Barry Sanders, Jim Abbott, Ken Griffey, Jr., and Patrick Ewing for Children's Press.

Reiser and his wife, Adrienne, live in New York. They have four grown children (Philip, Helene, Steven, and Stuart) and two grandchildren (Nechemiah and Naftali).